YES to BLESSED

30 Devotions to **BOLD FAITH, BEATING FEAR,** and **BIG ACTION** for **GEN-Z**

KIHRYN KHA

Copyright © 2023 Kihryn Kha

ISBN: 978-1-955362-16-0

All rights reserved. No portion of this book may be reproduced in any form without written permission from the publisher or author, except as permitted by U.S. copyright law.

Although both the publisher and author have used reasonable care in preparing this book, the information it contains is distributed "as is" and without warranties of any kind. This book is not intended as legal, financial, or health advice, and not all of the recommendations will be suitable for your situation. Professional legal, financial, and health advisors should be consulted, as needed. Neither the publisher nor the author shall be liable for any costs, expenses, or damages resulting from the use of or reliance on the information contained in this book.

All Scripture quotations, unless otherwise indicated, are taken from the Holy Bible, New International Version®, NIV®. Copyright ©1973, 1978, 1984, 2011 by Biblica, Inc.™ Used by permission of Zondervan. All rights reserved worldwide. www.zondervan.com The "NIV" and "New International Version" are trademarks registered in the United States Patent and Trademark Office by Biblica, Inc.™

Published by

STORY ꙮ CHORUS

Learn more at www.StoryChorus.com.

Dedication

First, to the One that made it all come together and put this dream inside of me: God. I thank Him for choosing me, I thank Him for giving me the platforms I have to share with others. He gave me a vision and was there with me through the whole process!

Next, I want to dedicate this book to my parents. All of the late-night convos, tears cried, and laughs and memories we've made have brought me to where I am today. You two have always been the people I look up to! Thank you for teaching me to be a Yeser!

I also want to dedicate this to my sister. You are my best friend and always there to go on drives and get late-night food with. Thank you for always showing me what pushing through and being a fighter looks like. You may be my younger sister, but you have taught me more than you will ever know!

Now I want to talk to all my Gen Z friends—this book is dedicated to you too! You were made to say yes to the opportunities God has laid before you. You were made to make big moves. God has put you in this world to break down walls built up for years. Never underestimate what a difference our generation can make!

Last but not least, I want to thank the Story Chorus team! Thanks for seeing a 16-year-old girl wanting to change the world and believing in her. Thank you for saying yes and giving me a chance to prove what God has put inside of me! For that, I will always be grateful!

And to all the people in the beginning, middle, and end. Thank you for being my cheerleaders through it all. Thank you for constantly reminding me I could do it even when I may have stopped believing in myself!

Let's go change the world!

Table of Contents

	Ready to Say Yes?!. ix
Day One	Why *Yes to Blessed*? 1
Day Two	The Yes Cycle. 5
Day Three	What Does "Christian" Mean? 9
Day Four	Be Courageous. 13
Day Five	Being a Little Bit Salty 17
Day Six	One of One 21
Day Seven	Love? 25
Day Eight	Your Opportunities Are Endless! 29
Day Nine	Simple Obedience Changes History!. 33
Day Ten	Don't Give Up! 39
Day Eleven	I'm Done with Excuses 43
Day Twelve	Consumer or Creator? 47
Day Thirteen	Famous for What?. 51

Day Fourteen	Do You Have a Voice?	55
Day Fifteen	How Do You Fight?	59
Day Sixteen	Be a Warrior for God!	63
Day Seventeen	It's Okay to Be a Little Spicy!	67
Day Eighteen	Peasants to Royalty	71
Day Nineteen	My Love for Worship Music	75
Day Twenty	Your Gifts Are from God	79
Day Twenty-One	It's Time to Sparkle	83
Day Twenty-Two	My Mom and Dad	87
Day Twenty-Three	You're Going to Have Haters	91
Day Twenty-Four	You Can't Do Life Alone	95
Day Twenty-Five	I Am Still Here	99
Day Twenty-Six	He Found Favor	103
Day Twenty-Seven	Speak Him	107
Day Twenty-Eight	It Is Time to Multiply	111
Day Twenty-Nine	Dripping with the Flavor of God!	115
Day Thirty	Your Final Exercise!	119
	About the Author	123

Ready to Say Yes?!

Hey, readers! You're probably wondering, "Who is this girl?" Well, I'm Kihryn Kha, a 16-year-old girl from a little town called Zanesville, Ohio. I used to struggle with speaking up, but God has been helping me find my voice over the past couple of years.

He's spoken to me in dreams, showing me visions of speaking and writing a devotional. At first, I doubted I could do it. But here's the thing: I used to be so scared to share this part of my life. What if it doesn't make sense to anyone else? What if I don't actually know what to say? What if I don't know enough because I'm only 16?!

Have you ever felt like this? Like God wants you to do something or say something. But then it feels really scary. Like a voice saying, "Who are YOU to think God will use you?"

Guess what? If you've felt like this too, you're not alone. Have you ever heard of a young pastor named Timothy in the Bible?

He was like a son to the Apostle Paul. So when Timothy was feeling just like this, Paul told him in 1 Timothy 4:12, "Don't let anyone look down on you because you are young, but set an example for the believers in speech, in conduct, in love, in faith and in purity."

Woah. Even pastors in the Bible were afraid they couldn't be who God made them to be! I think it's amazing. And it inspires me to totally surrender myself, my fears, and my feelings to God.

I still have to work on my courage every day—I'm not perfect. But God is, and through Him, I can do anything. And guess what? So can you!

Now, I'm all in—fully committed to saying YES to God and entering His Kingdom BOLDLY. Just like Timothy who God used to set the example for people older than him. No one can dim my sparkle for Him. Even some of the people in my life don't get my deep longing for more and my desire to live an abundant life for Him. But that's okay! As long as God and I understand, that's what really counts 😘.

In this book, I've structured my devotionals to build on each other. So, let's journey together, saying yes to the blessings God has for us. I'm still learning every day, just like you. Can't wait for you to dive in!

Let's get started.

BOLD *faith*  BIG *action*

Day One

Why Yes to Blessed?

==" Blessed rather are those who hear the word of God and obey it."==

LUKE 11:28

I was lying down one night and God revealed to me what He wanted me to name this devotional: *Yes to Blessed.*

Saying yes to what God has called me to do is something I struggle with. I had to really have faith in God's process.

The blessing comes after the yes. When you say yes to God, He promises a blessing from your obedience. 2 Corinthians 1:20 says, "For all the promises of God find their Yes in him. That is why it is through him that we utter our Amen to God for his glory."

I have had to say yes to a lot of things in my life. And if I had not said yes to God, I would not be in the position I am today and able to write this! I wouldn't have had confidence in myself, although I am still working on the confidence part 😉.

A Bible story I often think about is when Peter was out all night fishing and did not catch anything. Peter was discouraged, but Jesus told him to go back out and fish from the other side of the boat. Jesus asked for Peter's obedience, his yes. When Peter said yes, he caught a lot of fish. God blessed him for being obedient.

God is so good! It makes me happy to live my life with Him! So let's partner with God and choose to say yes.

WHY *YES TO BLESSED*?

LET'S GET REAL.

- *What is something in life you struggle with where you have to trust God's process?*
- *What blessings have you experienced after being obedient to God?*

BOLD *faith* BIG *action*

Day Two

The Yes Cycle

> "Since, then, we have such a hope, we act with great boldness."

2 CORINTHIANS 3:12

In October of 2022, I had the opportunity to speak in my Bible class at Valor Global Online School. I spoke about Mary and something I call the Yes Cycle. I talked about Mary's obedience and how she walked in God's favor. This pattern is what I mean by the Yes Cycle.

When you act in obedience, you open up the ability to walk in God's favor. When you say yes to God, you start walking in the favor of God. When you are walking in the favor of God, the devil cannot take you out of the favor God has assigned you. When you start opening up the door for God and saying yes, God's provision falls all over your life.

There are times in life when we need to take a step forward and say yes to God's calling! It is not easy to say yes. It takes a lot of faith and boldness.

2 Corinthians 3:12 says, "Since, then, we have such a hope, we act with great boldness."

I think that message is so good! When we say yes, we need to act in great boldness—not just boldness but *great* boldness.

There are key people in the Bible who said yes to God, even when it wasn't easy, and acted with great boldness.

When God called Moses to lead the Israelites out of Egypt, Moses initially hesitated and questioned his ability to speak effectively. However, God gave Moses the courage and boldness to approach Pharaoh and demand the release of His people[1].

Esther was a Jewish woman who became the queen of Persia. When she learned that her people were going to be exterminated, she acted with boldness and

---

[1] Exodus 3–4

approached the king, even though it was against the law to do so without being summoned. Esther risked her own life to save her people and was used by God to deliver them from destruction[2].

Moses and Esther are inspirations to act with great boldness in obedience to God. They heard what God was telling them and they said yes! If you can do the same, you will start walking in God's favor and no one can remove you from that favor. This message is vital in being able to grow!

LET'S GET REAL.

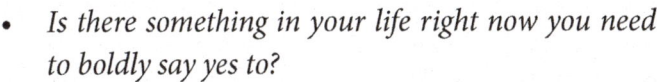

Spill the tea:

- *Is there something in your life right now you need to boldly say yes to?*
- *What is your calling from God and how can you say yes?*

---

[2] Esther 4

BOLD *faith*  BIG *action*

Day Three

What Does "Christian" Mean?

> "Each of you should use whatever gift you have received to serve others, as faithful stewards of God's grace in its various forms."

1 PETER 4:10

Do you know what the word "Christian" means?

"Christian" means "little Christ". When the word "Christian" first started being used, it was probably meant as an insult or at least a nickname that wasn't very nice. Peter actually says not to be "ashamed" if they are called Christians[3].

---

[3] 1 Peter 4:16

But what does being a Christian, or a "little Christ", mean in the world today? God put you on this earth as a little Christ. If you say you're a Christan, then you were made to spread the Word. We are supposed to be a little Christ to a world that is longing for Him.

No one can ever *be* Jesus, but we can try to be *like* Him. What I mean is treat people like Jesus would have treated them and show them His love. They might not know it, but everyone in this world longs to be loved and seen. When we are in God's presence, we are loved, we are seen. That's what it means to be a Christian today, to bring people into God's presence by being a "little Christ".

When I think of biblical figures who portray this, I think of the disciples. In Acts 1:8, Jesus says, "But you will receive power when the Holy Spirit comes on you, and you will be my witnesses in Jerusalem, and in all Judea and Samaria, and to the ends of the earth."

He wanted His disciples to go all over the world and share the Word. That is why God hand-picked the disciples and they "recruited more". And look at our world now! People are coming to know Christ because of others showing them what it looks like to be a Christian.

WHAT DOES "CHRISTIAN" MEAN?

Why do we shy back, why do we think we are not enough, and why do we put fear above what God has literally called us to do? I believe it is because we think we are not good enough. But if God literally names us little Christ, then He is always going to have us in the palm of His hand.

So step out with confidence! Treat people and yourself like Jesus would. And love others like Jesus loved the world.

LET'S GET REAL.

Spill the tea: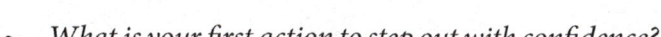

- *What is your first action to step out with confidence?*
- *How can you be a "little Christ" for others today?*

Day Four

Be Courageous

> "Be strong and courageous. Do not be afraid or terrified because of them, for the Lord your God goes with you; he will never leave you nor forsake you."

DEUTERONOMY 31:6

Did you know the word "courage" is used around 35 times in the Bible? I'll be honest, I did not know that! Clearly, God is trying to teach us a little bit more about being courageous. In Joshua 1:6-9, God tells us: "Be strong and very courageous. Be careful to obey all the law my servant Moses gave you; do not turn from it to the right or to the left, that you may be successful wherever you go. Keep this Book of the Law always on your lips; meditate on it day and night, so that you may be careful to do everything written in it. Then you will be prosperous and successful.

> Have I not commanded you? Be strong and courageous. Do not be afraid; do not be discouraged, for the Lord your God will be with you wherever you go."

Let's break this down a little. Within this passage, it talks multiple times about being strong and courageous; do not turn to the left or right, let the law always be on your lips, again be strong and courageous, do not be afraid, do not be discouraged, and wherever you go God will be with you.

When I read this, I can't stop thinking about how good God is.

Let's think of our bodies for a second. For example, the human skeleton is not very pretty. But when we add everything that we are to that skeleton, it is a beautiful picture. Your life is like that skeleton; it's not beautiful on its own. But when we add Jesus to our life, He makes it beautiful. Jesus creates that beautiful picture from something not very pretty because He is the most important part.

That is what this verse means to me. Jesus brings strength and beauty. And He will always be there for us. When we believe we are made beautiful by Jesus, it makes us more courageous because we know we were made perfectly in His image.

BE COURAGEOUS

LET'S GET REAL.

- *How can you practice stepping out with courage? What are things in your life where you can drop others' opinions and choose courage?*

- *In what areas of your life do you need to trust in God so He can make what you're walking through beautiful?*

Day Five

Being a Little Bit Salty

> "You are the salt of the earth. But if the salt loses its saltiness, how can it be made salty again? It is no longer good for anything, except to be thrown out and trampled underfoot."

MATTHEW 5:13

Salty? When someone asks, "Why are you so salty?" it's normally a negative thing. But Matthew 5:13 says we are the salt of the earth, which is a positive thing!

What does salt do? When we put salt on food, we do it to enhance the flavor. When we walk into a room, we can be the salt of the earth by enhancing the negative or the positive. We have to decide if we will bring the positive or the negative to any situation.

Let me be honest with you: if you want to enhance the negative, then it will be harder for you to find a positive community to lean on. If people are trying to better themselves, they will not want your negativity in their life.

I have had people in my life that are just so heavy to be around because all they do is talk about the negatives in their lives. But let's talk about the positive flavor! I believe there can be more positive than negative in the world. When we choose to be positive, we bring lightness to a room. When we choose positivity, we are choosing light.

The next verse, Matthew 5:14, says, "You are the light of the world. A town built on a hill cannot be hidden." I was at my school retreat, and the room was dark, but we had our flashlights on in a circle. We were the light of the world. And that is what positivity looks like. A positive person can light up a dark room.

So, as the salt of the earth, let's all agree to enhance the positive flavor. And as the light of the world, let's show people what it's like to live life being that light.

BEING A LITTLE BIT SALTY

LET'S GET REAL.

- *Are there people in your life that try to enhance the negative flavor? What can you do about that?*
- *What is the next situation you can be the light in?*

Day Six

One of One

> "Your eyes saw my unformed body;
> all the days ordained for me were written
> in your book before one of them came to be."

PSALM 139:16

You are one of one! There is no one else like you in this world. You were made beautifully and wonderfully. God put so much time and thought into creating you. You were put on this Earth for a reason. God put you here for one of one reason, and He has known that reason since before you were born.

These are all biblical references, not just worldly sayings. God is calling you *up* and *out*.

Recently at church, our pastor was talking about the difference between good and great. The devil wants you only to be good. "Good" is not a threat to him. But being great is a threat. You were created by God, as one of one, to be great.

When I think of someone created for one of one reason, I think about Mary. God chose her to do something no one else could do. He called her up and out to be great. I think that is a beautiful representation of being one of one. God has a specific plan for each of us, and that plan involves a great purpose.

You can not stop someone who is great. So many of us get distracted by being good enough when we need to be trying for greatness. Instead of being good kids, good parents, good grandparents, and good friends, we should try to be great in every area. When we want to be great, then what we do will be great. When we strive to be great, then we start growing, speaking life over ourselves, and living more abundantly. Remember, we all have the potential to be great because we are one of one, wonderfully made by God.

LET'S GET REAL.

- *What makes you one of one?*
- *In what areas of your life do you need to try to be great, not just good?*

Day Seven

Love?

> "I give you a new commandment: Love each other. Just as I have loved you, so you also must love each other. This is how everyone will know that you are my disciples when you love each other."

JOHN 13:34

Many of us have different meanings of what love actually is. People love in different ways. That is why the idea of love languages was created.

I grew up in a family that is very loving to one another but not in a touchy type of way. We all know we love each other without having to touch often! Other people in my life approach things differently. They would make sure to hug me and say they loved me, but the actual love behind the touch and the words wasn't something I truly felt. Personally, I am not a very touchy person, but I have learned there are different ways to show love. There is both verbal and physical love.

In the Bible, God says multiple times to love as He does. John 13:34–35 is one of the most well know of these instances:

"I give you a new commandment: Love each other. Just as I have loved you, so you also must love each other. This is how everyone will know that you are my disciples when you love each other."

So how do we love like God loves? The more I started going to different places, the more I saw how others treated people. I saw how their way of loving was different, especially when I went to Arizona. Their love was truly like Jesus' love. It was warm and inviting. The first thing you see is their smile. They shared welcoming words and then a hug. And even though I am not a touchy person, I appreciated their hugs. I could feel God's love through them.

A hug is not a bad thing, but a hug does not mean *a thing* without true love behind it. You can hug people all you want, but if it is not a love-filled hug, it has *no* purpose. I have experienced a loving hug, and it

LOVE?

brought tears to my eyes! There are people in my life who don't often say they love you or give many hugs. But when they do, it has meaning!

Let your love make people know you really mean it! Let your love be a reflection of God's love.

When I tell people I love them, I always mean it. I would get hit by a train for them. I am not just throwing out the words. When I say it, I want it to have meaning.

If you are reading this, I love you with the true love of God!

LET'S GET REAL.

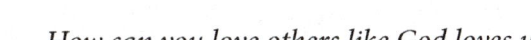

Spill the tea:

- *How can you love others like God loves us?*
- *What are some ways you can show people you love them, besides words and hugs?*

Day Eight

Your Opportunities Are Endless!

> "Therefore, as we have opportunity, let us do good to all people, especially to those who belong to the family of believers."

GALATIANS 6:10

You, beautiful people, have *opportunities*!

You have goals and places you want to go, but you're not sure if you can reach them. There were times when I didn't think I could write this devotional. I just did not think I had what it took. But God put me on this Earth for impact! And He put you here for that too!

To reach your goals and seize your opportunities, you have to show up for yourself, for God, for your family, and for the people around you! They need you, I need you, and my kids are going to need your kids. Show these people what boldness looks like. Show them how to show up and show out for God!

When I think of the Bible and people seizing their opportunities, I think of both Joseph and Peter.

When Joseph was sold into slavery by his jealous brothers, he could have given up hope. Instead, he seized the opportunity to use his God-given gifts of interpreting dreams and managing resources to become a trusted advisor to the Pharaoh of Egypt. He could have given up and said life was just too hard, but he chose to rise up.

When Jesus called Peter to follow Him, he left his fishing business behind and embarked on a new journey. Despite his doubts and failures, Peter continued to seize opportunities to share the message of Jesus with others. Peter could have turned away to do his own thing, but instead, he took the road less traveled and chose to follow Jesus and spread His message.

We all have opportunities to follow Jesus, but often we are too busy making excuses. Do you get caught up in

YOUR OPPORTUNITIES ARE ENDLESS!

telling yourself why you can't and why you shouldn't and why this and why that? If so, it's time to just do the dang thing! Don't make any more excuses!

I know it can be hard. I made multiple excuses about why I was not qualified to write this devotional. I didn't see how God could use my story to help others. But when I decided to stop making excuses, I finally started writing, which has been so rewarding in the end!

LET'S GET REAL.

Spill the tea:

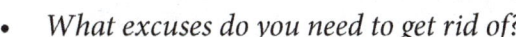

- *What excuses do you need to get rid of?*
- *What opportunities do you need to take?*

Day Nine

Simple Obedience Changes History!

==*"And this is love: that we walk in obedience to his commands. As you have heard from the beginning, his command is that you walk in love."*==

2 JOHN 1:6

In late 2022, I was at a worship night in California, and we were singing a song about giving God our yes. The song's lyrics were, "Simple obedience changes history." That is so true! I didn't even know this song existed, but tears started rolling down my face when they began singing. This is a choice we all have to make over and over again: will we be obedient?

When my parents told me we were moving, I resisted for months. I did not understand why they felt called to move. Why would God ever want me to leave the place I knew so well? Eventually, I had to accept that moving was happening, and I had to go.

Today, I can see why God wanted us to leave. I have had doors open for me that I never even dreamed of. I have made more connections with people than I ever had before. God has renewed my thoughts for bigger and better thinking. The simple obedience of accepting that we had to move changed my history.

I believe that I can help change history in the name of Jesus because of my obedience.

The next verse of that worship song was about the harvest being ripe and how we are ready *now* to bear fruit for Jesus. The song was saying we need to stop waiting because the fruit is *already* ripe. While I listened to the song, I was just filled with emotion because it felt like God was telling me I needed to give Him my obedience and change history. He was telling me that my fruit was ripe, and I couldn't let it spoil!

When I think about obedience changing history, I think of Moses. God wanted him to lead the Israelites. He said yes, and it changed history! Hebrews 11:27–29 shows us how Moses lived his faith and continued saying yes and being obedient to God:

"By faith he left Egypt, not fearing the king's anger; he persevered because he saw him who is invisible. By faith he kept the Passover and the application of blood, so that the destroyer of the firstborn would not touch the firstborn of Israel. By faith the people passed through the Red Sea as on dry land; but when the Egyptians tried to do so, they were drowned."

This verse uses the words "by faith" over and over. That is what obedience means. Relying on faith and saying yes to God even when things are difficult like they were for Moses.

So today, I want to remind you that obedience can change history! Your fruit is ripe! It's time to harvest that fruit and not let it spoil. I encourage you to look at some areas in your life where you need to have simple obedience, and it will change your history!

LET'S GET REAL.

 Spill the tea:

- *What is your next act of simple obedience that can change history?*
- *What fruit do you need to harvest in your life right now?*

Day Ten

Don't Give Up!

> "Let us not become weary in doing good, for at the proper time we will reap a harvest if we do not give up."

GALATIANS 6:9

God has the best life planned for you. But you will still have struggles, doubts, and fears. Don't give up!

You have the choice to push through, pray, and rely on God. Or you can give up and not let God show up for you! God wants to lead you all the time, even when you don't want to be led. When we are able to trust God and lean into what He is trying to show us, living life with Him is a lot easier. Jesus wants you to win! But you also need to be 100% in! It takes Jesus, but it also takes you! You can't expect Jesus to come though if you are not willing to do your part.

You need to cast out the words "I can't" and replace them with "I can". As it says in Philippians 4:13, "I can do all things through Christ who gives me strength."

I can!

Not many people know this, but I was a gymnast from the ages of three to ten. I was good, and I trained with some of the best gymnasts in the world. Training with the best means you have to take on some skills that are really scary. I remember the first time I did a back tuck on the balance beam. A beam is four inches wide and doesn't leave a lot of room for messing up. I could have slipped, and something awful could have happened. But I kept going, telling myself, "I can! I can!" Gymnastics was a part of my life where I learned to say "I can" over and over again until I believed it. There is something about telling yourself "I can" that makes you so much more confident to do scary things.

So let's agree to push through and win for God. Share your testimony because people need to hear it. And don't give up, because God has the best life planned for you!

LET'S GET REAL.

- *In what areas of your life do you need to replace "I can't" with "I can"?*
- *How can you do your part to win for God today?*

BOLD *faith*  BIG *action*

Day Eleven

I'm Done with Excuses

> "Don't let anyone look down on you because you are young, but set an example for the believers in speech, in conduct, in love, in faith and in purity."

2 TIMOTHY 4:12

I am done hearing everybody's excuses! I can't because…

I'm too busy…

I have a job…

I'm too young…

I'm too old…

The excuses I dislike the most are "I am too old" or "I am too young." In the Bible, God used young and old people. Mary was fifteen or sixteen when she had Jesus. Sara was very old when she became pregnant with her son. I have been around teenagers who are living in their purpose for Jesus. You're never too young to follow Jesus and find your purpose! Just look at Paul's commission to Timothy in 1 Timothy 4:12, "Don't let anyone look down on you because you are young, but set an example for the believers in speech, in conduct, in love, in faith and in purity." He's saying that young people should step up even though we could be overlooked or not taken seriously. Being young is not a reason to withhold from stepping up and setting a standard.

I also know older people who say it's too late to start something new. You're never too old to start! You need to be living your purpose until you take your last breath.

Stop making excuses about why you can't do something. If you are reading this then you are still alive, and God has plans for you. So let's stop making excuses and live for Jesus!

I'M DONE WITH EXCUSES

LET'S GET REAL.

- *Has being "too young" or "too old" ever been an excuse for you? How can you let that go?*

- *How can you encourage others to let go of excuses by living for Jesus?*

BOLD *faith*  BIG *action*

Day Twelve

Consumer or Creator?

> "Do everything without grumbling and arguing so that you may be blameless and pure, innocent children of God surrounded by people who are crooked and corrupt. Among these people you shine like stars in the world."
>
> **PHILIPPIANS 2:14–15**

In life, you can be a consumer or a creator. You can take from God or create with God. You can just consume what people say, or you can take what people say and create something from it. You can lay around and watch movies, or you can get up and go and create something amazing. You can sit and read your Bible and never do anything with the teachings, or you can go tell people about God and call out their greatness with the Bible story you just read.

So many people want to sit around and watch television but also receive a blessing. They want more money and nicer things, but they also just want to consume. They don't want to create those things for themselves. You are not going to get the blessing if you are not creating anything to support that blessing!

It's okay to watch television sometimes and have relaxing days. Everyone needs a rest day! But don't complain when you have responsibilities to carry. We need to give God respect for His Word. If we only read it and keep it to ourselves, we are not giving His Word the respect it deserves. We need to share it with people who need it!

LET'S GET REAL.

Spill the tea:

- *Are you consuming God or creating with God?*
- *How can you be a better co-creator with God?*

BOLD *faith*  BIG *action*

Day Thirteen

Famous for What?

> "Therefore go and make disciples of all nations, baptizing them in the name of the Father and of the Son and of the Holy Spirit, and teaching them to obey everything I have commanded you. And surely I am with you always, to the very end of the age."

MATTHEW 28:19–20

We live in a culture where everyone wants to be famous. Right now, I want you to write down on a piece of paper why you might want to be famous.

Most of us would probably say we want to be famous so we can have more money, or have a big house, or know other famous people. I recently read a book by Sadie Robertson called *Who Are You Following?* and she had a chapter about this subject. I thought it was such a great thing to think about! So, I started really thinking about what I wanted to be famous for, and I realized the reason I want to be famous is to make Jesus famous!

I'm not saying this to make myself look better than anyone! If you did not write that as your reason for wanting to be famous, that is okay! I also had different reasons when I first started thinking about it, but God came to me and told me that He put me in this world to share Him with other people. God wants us to share Him with everyone!

"Therefore go and make disciples of all nations, baptizing them in the name of the Father and of the Son and of the Holy Spirit, and teaching them to obey everything I have commanded you. And surely I am with you always, to the very end of the age." Matthew 28:19–20

Wanting to be famous doesn't have to seem like a negative thing. It doesn't have to be about getting rich or having the nicest things. Being famous can be used for greatness, like spreading the Word of God! It is so fulfilling to spread the Word of God. You don't have to be a preacher to make Jesus famous. It is something we can do in our everyday lives. We can practice loving like Jesus and extending His grace. There are so many things we can be the hands and the feet of Jesus for!

LET'S GET REAL.

- *Do you need to change your reasons for wanting to be famous?*
- *How could you use fame to spread God's Word?*

Day Fourteen

Do You Have a Voice?

> "That I might sing praises to you and not be silent. O Lord my God, I will give you thanks forever!"
>
> **PSALM 30:12**

Do you have a voice? You are probably like, "Well, yes I have a voice. I talk to people!"

But let's really think about this. Do you truly have a voice? Do people know who you are in the way you want to be known?

I used to be someone who would just do whatever I was told. If someone had an idea, I would agree with them, even if it wasn't what I wanted. Some of you might think, "Ooh, that's a good thing!" But it was really just letting people boss me around.

When I changed schools to Valor Global Online, my advocate, Mrs. Kim, helped me change this. She taught me how to use my voice as a tool. She explained to me that God gave me a voice to use and not just to let people walk all over me.

How do you want to be known? Do you want to just accept what others say and get bossed around? Or do you want to use your voice and add value to any room you are in? You get put in rooms for impact. If you are in the room, then make it known in a good way! Use your voice to have an impact on other people.

You might have read this and thought, "Yes, I have a voice and I use it."

But are you using your voice for impact? Your voice is a tool from God, so make sure to use it wisely!

DO YOU HAVE A VOICE?

LET'S GET REAL.

- *Are you using your God-given voice for impact?*
- *Are there times in your life you need to choose to use your voice?*

BOLD *faith*  BIG *action*

Day Fifteen

How Do You Fight?

> "Submit yourselves therefore to God.
> Resist the devil, and he will flee from you."

JAMES 4:7

I have had to learn to fight in prayer.

If you have never watched the movie War Room you need to go watch it now! It's a great example of how we need to fight through prayer. One of the main characters had her own "war room" where she prayed for hours. She was a woman that prayed through everything. And she was able to influence the people around her to do the same.

Life is not always going to be easy. In fact, it's going to get really hard sometimes. It might be easy to think that, when things get hard, if you are a Christian, then God is just going to heal you or fix the hard situation. But that's not how it works! God wants to step in during our tough times, but if you are not fighting and doing your part then that's not going to happen. You have to partner with God.

What does it look like to partner with God to fight?

It looks like getting down on your knees, putting your hands up, and crying out to God. It's giving God all you have; praying over your room and all your stuff. Spiritually fighting is giving everything over to God. It's showing God you fully surrender to His plan and His will.

And don't forget the falling on your face and thanking Him! Don't take God's love for granted!

HOW DO YOU FIGHT?

LET'S GET REAL.

- *What spiritual battles are you fighting?*
- *How can you partner with God to better fight your battles?*

Day Sixteen

Be a Warrior for God!

> "Through you we push back our enemies; through your name we trample our foes."

PSALM 44:5

At church one morning, someone asked to pray over me and I said "Absolutely!" He prophesied that I was a warrior for God, so I had to dive in to see what that really meant.

When I started looking into what it means to be a warrior for God, these things kept coming up:

- Warriors are equipped for battle!
- Warriors use their wisdom!

- Warriors are strong!
- Warriors have experience!
- Warriors are with God!

Being a warrior for God means rising to challenges. In my life, I have had to rise to some challenges. When I was a gymnast, I had hernia surgery and had to take a lot of time off, which was very hard. I have had surgery on both of my ears. I was almost deaf in one ear, and the other ear had a paralyzed bone. Because of these challenges I have faced, God is using my story. I have embraced my challenges and risen up.

Since the day she was born, my sister has shown me what being a warrior for God looks like. She has had to rise up in a lot of scenarios in her life, and I have been able to watch her bloom through every single one. It is not my story to share, so someday I hope she will share her story with you. But I wanted to honor her because she is a walking miracle!

Life is not always going to be easy. But when we live our life with God, He uses our challenges to help us grow.

Have you been prophesied over? If you have, I want you to think about the word that was spoken over

BE A WARRIOR FOR GOD!

you and look up its biblical meaning. There is a reason God told that person to speak that over you. Walk in it! I took the time to look into being a warrior for God and it allowed me to see how my challenges have helped me grow.

Even if you have not had a word spoken over you, I am asking you to *rise up*! There is a calling on your life and it's time to respond!

LET'S GET REAL.

Spill the tea:

- *What challenges have you overcome?*
- *How has God helped you grow and rise up through those challenges?*

Day Seventeen

It's Okay to Be a Little Spicy!

> "I am sending you out like sheep among wolves. Therefore be as shrewd as snakes and as innocent as doves."

MATTHEW 10:16

Mrs. Kim, my amazing advocate at school, helped me realize it's okay to stand up for myself. She showed me it's okay to be a little spicy! Mrs. Kim is spicy (in a good way). When I have a problem with a teacher, classmate, or teammate, I talk to Mrs. Kim about it. She always tells me to be polite but kinda spicy! So what does that look like?

Well, when you start using your voice for impact, there will be some haters. I had some! When I started using my voice, someone told me that she liked the old Kihryn. The version of me who did not talk and just let people walk all over her. I took that as a compliment because it meant my voice was being heard! I came back with a polite but kinda spicy answer for her.

I also had someone in school make fun of me for my shoes and for having good grades. He said the only reason I bought shoes was to flex them on Instagram and that I was a nerdy kid for having good grades. I am grateful that I learned from Mrs. Kim how to respond in a polite but kinda spicy way, and I was able to stand up for myself (I also blocked him because that negative person did not need to see my stuff)!

I will not let people being rude to me change what I know God says about me. It is time to stand up for *you*! So, thank you to these classmates for helping me learn how to stand up for myself! And thank you, Mrs. Kim, for your help in making me a polite but kinda spicy girl!

Daniel 3:16–18 caught my eye when I was thinking about standing up for myself. I love how Shadrach,

IT'S OKAY TO BE A LITTLE SPICY!

Meshach, and Abednego knew what was right and stood up for it and themselves!

"Shadrach, Meshach and Abednego replied to him, 'King Nebuchadnezzar, we do not need to defend ourselves before you in this matter. If we are thrown into the blazing furnace, the God we serve is able to deliver us from it, and he will deliver us from Your Majesty's hand. But even if he does not, we want you to know, Your Majesty, that we will not serve your gods or worship the image of gold you have set up.'"

Often in life, we know what is right, and we want to do what is right. But it can be hard to stand up to our own King Nebuchadnezzar. When you're in these situations, remember that it is okay to be a little spicy!

LET'S GET REAL.

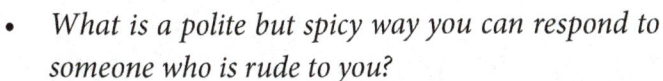

- *What is a polite but spicy way you can respond to someone who is rude to you?*
- *In what ways can you use your spice?*

Day Eighteen

Peasants to Royalty

> "You will also be a crown of beauty in the hand of the Lord, And a royal diadem in the hand of your God."
>
> **ISAIAH 62:3**

Do you believe you are worthy of the throne God wants to give you? One of my favorite quotes from Pastor Dave Ross is, "What good is it if your bloodline is of kings, but you choose to live the life of peasants because you don't believe you're worthy of the throne?"

This worthiness is something I have struggled with and so have other people I know, including my mom. She never felt comfortable sharing what God told her to share with the world. She lived a very behind-the-scenes life for a long time. My mom is someone I have always looked up to, and I always had a sad heart when she did not feel worthy of what God had given her.

In August of 2022, my mom was asked to speak at a Massive Momentum event and she said yes! Even after saying yes, she doubted herself and I was like, "Mom, you got this!" The night she got up on stage and spoke, there was so much happiness in my heart for her. When I saw that she did it, I knew I could do it too! God had told me that I was going to speak, and I had a hard time believing it. But He used my mom to show me I could do it too.

We are all called to the throne, but many times we are not living like we are worthy of that throne. You are royal. You are higher than the rest because God is with you. Know your worth in God and start walking in your royalty!

LET'S GET REAL.

- *Are you holding yourself back because you don't feel worthy?*
- *How can you start to live out your royal calling?*

Day Nineteen

My Love for Worship Music

> "I will sing to the LORD all my life;
> I will sing praise to my God as long as I live."

PSALM 104:33

I love worship music! Whenever I listen to worship music, I can feel God. I can feel His presence around me.

It's hard for me to explain the feeling, but everyone has a way we feel good. When I hear worship music, I feel ready to conquer the world. I am always reminded that He made me perfectly, and that is where my confidence comes from.

Have you ever gotten goosebumps while listening to worship music? Did you know those goosebumps are the Holy Spirit? Someone told me that and I was like "Oh my Lanta, that is crazy!" because I always get goosebumps when listening to worship music, especially in the car by myself. My mom has started playing worship music in our house right when we wake up. It sets the atmosphere for the day and welcomes the Holy Spirit into our home.

Playing this music shows that we want God in our home, we desire His presence. I think worship music is a really good motivator because when you listen to songs about how good God is, it makes you want to be better and go share his Word.

Below are some of my favorite worship songs! I encourage you to start listening to them and sharing them with your family. Show everyone that you desire God's presence in your home through this beautiful music!

MY LOVE FOR WORSHIP MUSIC

LET'S GET REAL.

 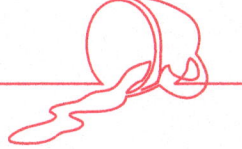

- *Where can you start using worship music?*
- *How can it help in your daily life?*

BOLD *faith* 👓 BIG *action*

Day Twenty

Your Gifts Are from God

> "Each of you should use whatever gift you have received to serve others, as faithful stewards of God's grace in its various forms."
>
> **1 PETER 4:10**

For years, I told everyone that I would never be a speaker. It was not one of my gifts. I was a shy person, and I never considered that speaking might be one of my gifts from God.

Then, in January 2022, I was given a vision about speaking on stage. My first reaction was, "Ummm, no, God." He showed it to me again, and I still said, "No, God, I can't do that. I don't have the words."

When I finally shared these visions with my mom, she told me that saying no was a dishonor to God. I needed to own that gift and share it!

So, one evening at a worship night, I got down on my knees and said, "God, I will speak on a stage because I know that You have called me to that. I re-give You my life because I don't want to operate on my gifts but on Your gifts."

When I think of God-given gifts, I immediately think of Moses. He was picked to lead the Israelites, but he did not think he had the right gifts to do it. God said He would provide. I believe He is saying that to all of us! Step into your calling, and God will provide for you.

I challenge you to get on your knees, talk to God about your gifts, and tell Him you are committed to loving *all* the gifts He's given you! Let Him know that you are ready to use the ones that you may not love as much. Tell Him you know there is a reason you have them!

Go show the world what God gave you!

YOUR GIFTS ARE FROM GOD

LET'S GET REAL.

- *What is a God-given gift you have that you are reluctant to use?*

- *What is an action step towards using that gift from God?*

Day Twenty-One

It's Time to Sparkle

> "Now may the God of hope fill you with all joy and peace in believing, that you may abound in hope by the power of the Holy Spirit."
>
> **ROMANS 15:13**

Last Thanksgiving, I was with my family in Tennessee. I was having a wonderful time, and I was in such a great mood. We were shopping for Black Friday deals, and I was so happy and joyful—I was sparkling! But it came to my attention that some people did not understand why I was acting that way. They were questioning my sparkle.

It made me wonder why it seems more normal for people to be grumpy and angry instead of happy. When we have to wait in line, or food is wrong at a restaurant, or something is not what we thought, most people immediately yell or get mad at others. But if we are treating people that way, then we are not showing them God's love and peace.

We need to start protecting our peace and not letting little things make us so mad. This is something that we work on a lot in our home. There are a lot of things in this world that are not peaceful, but Jesus can bring peace to any situation.

The Hebrew word for peace is "shalom." "Shalom" translates to completeness and wholeness. I think this is so cool because when Jesus gives us peace, it makes the situation complete and makes us feel whole. When we live in Jesus's peace, we can let go of little things that might make us angry and embrace our happiness and joy. We can sparkle!

IT'S TIME TO SPARKLE

LET'S GET REAL.

- *How can you protect your sparkle from dulling?*
- *What are some ways you can live more fully in Jesus's peace?*

Day Twenty-Two

My Mom and Dad

"Direct your children onto the right path, and when they are older, they will not leave it."

PROVERBS 22:6

As I was writing this devotional, I had to do an English assignment about a memoir. I picked one about my parent's relationship and felt I needed to write a chapter about it.

When my parents got married, they worked hard. They had me the year after getting married, so I witnessed a lot of their hard work throughout the years. It was not always easy for them, but they showed me how to get the work done. When I was younger, my mom worked all day and my dad worked at night. And some days my mom would work until midnight and my dad would work throughout the day. But growing up, my sister and I always had one of them with us. My mom and dad did all they could to make sure my sister and I were always taken care of. And eventually, my dad started his business and my mom was able to work with him too!

If you are a parent, I want you to know how beneficial it was for me to see my parents working hard and always trying to do better every day. If you are still a kid, try to find the good in what your parents do every day. They are trying their best and they love you, but you also have to show up with your best every day!

As teenagers, we can show younger kids what it looks like to be all in for Jesus. We can show them that they were created to do great things for the Kingdom and that what they say and do can have an impact on this world. No matter what age you are, I believe you can be a mentor to the people around you, just like my parents were for me.

Mom and Dad, thank you for showing up for me every day and showing me what it looks like to be brave, lean into the hard, and always follow God!

MY MOM AND DAD

LET'S GET REAL.

- *Who in your life are you looking up to?*
- *How can you be someone that others look up to?*

BOLD *faith* 👓 BIG *action*

Day Twenty-Three

You're Going to Have Haters

> "Let your light shine before others, that they may see your good deeds and glorify your Father in heaven."

MATTHEW 5:16

As I was driving the other day, I was thinking about the idea of how, in life, not everyone is going to like you. You might be saying, "Wow Kihryn, that's a little harsh." But it's a realization we all have to come to. Jesus had a lot of haters in His life, but He just kept chugging along and didn't care that there were people who didn't like Him.

Someone that embodies this for me is my dad. My dad has had a lot of haters, but he has always shown me that there are going to be people that don't like us and we can't worry about those people. We only need to care about what Jesus says!

Jesus says we need to be the light of the world. Can you hide light? No, you can't! It literally stands out wherever you go. When you start changing and doing big things, there are going to be people that don't like it. They will want you to hide your light. But we need to change that hate into an ever-brighter light!

So today, let's choose to not care what the haters think. Let's be a light for others to see the love of God!

LET'S GET REAL.

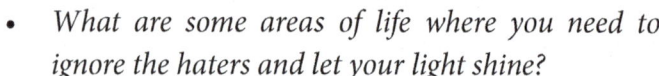
Spill the tea:

- *What are some areas of life where you need to ignore the haters and let your light shine?*
- *How will you respond when haters want to bring you down?*

Day Twenty-Four

You Can't Do Life Alone

> "For where two or three gather in my name, there am I with them."

MATTHEW 18:20

Late last year, as I was doing my Bible study, I came upon something that gave me a new perspective. The study I was doing was on Jesus's family tree. It walked through how God sent Jesus to us to forgive our sins.

The realization I came to is that God saw Adam after He created him, and He knew Adam could not do life alone. That is why He made Eve. If people in biblical times could not be alone, what makes us any different? Jesus knows we need a community to lean on in the good and bad times. People bring us up when we feel down, and we can also do that for others. We need to find the right community and pour into our relationships with them.

There have been so many times when I was reading the Bible, and this idea jumped out at me! One of the best examples is Matthew 18:20, which says, "For where two or three gather in my name, there am I with them." Jesus is telling us to be with people. We were not created to be by ourselves.

Jesus is so cool!

It's amazing how Jesus always shows us what to do before He has us do it. You just have to be willing to receive His message. Find your community and pour into it!

YOU CAN'T DO LIFE ALONE

LET'S GET REAL.

- *Do you have a community that supports you?*
- *How can you commit more fully to doing life with others?*

Day Twenty-Five

I Am Still Here

> "Even though I walk through the darkest valley, I will fear no evil, for you are with me; your rod and your staff, they comfort me."

PSALM 23:4

The other day, I was listening to a Christian song in the car, and the lyrics said, "You are still here." I loved that lyric!

At some point, all of us have struggled with fear. We've felt worn down and weak or lost our faith.

But you are still here! Jesus has not failed you yet.

There has not been one struggle where Jesus gave up on you. There has not been one time your situation

YES & BLESSED

was too hard for Him. You may be walking through something right now, but He has not stopped fighting for you. Don't lose hope. God is not done with you.

Get on your knees and remember all He has brought you through. Whatever your struggle, He has always been by your side, and He will not stop now.

Always remember you're still here ♥.

LET'S GET REAL.

- *What fears do you need to give to God?*
- *Where in your life do you need to remember you are still here?*

Day Twenty-Six

He Found Favor

"Noah however found favor with the Lord."

GENESIS 6:8

This year, I am working through the whole Bible and I was recently reading about Noah and the flood. As I was reading, the part I found so amazing was God's favor for Noah and how obedient Noah was to God to receive that favor.

In Genesis 6:17–19, God tells Noah exactly what is going to happen and what He needs Noah to do: "Look! I am about to cover the earth with a flood that will destroy every living thing that breathes. Everything on earth will die. But I will confirm my covenant with you. So enter the boat—you and your wife and your sons and their wives. Bring a pair of every kind of animal—a male and a female—into the boat with you to keep them alive during the flood."

Noah's obedience is so complete in this verse! God tells him what to do, and he doesn't question it. This took a lot of faith. It is not an overnight job to build an ark, fill it with these animals and enough food to survive a flood. And God knows that! It was going to be a hard job, but that is why God chose Noah and why Noah found favor with God.

God knew Noah's heart, and He also knows yours. He knows if you are going to wake up every day ready to pursue living for Him. He will always wait until the right time to give you a task, but then it is up to you to obey. No one can make that decision for you. We have a choice every day to make the right choices, look at the right things, and say the right words. You have to make your choices with intention.

God always fulfills His promises. If He said it, He will do it. And He expects the same from us!

LET'S GET REAL.

- *Are you ready to be obedient in the tasks God gives you?*

- *How can you make sure to fulfill your promises to God?*

BOLD *faith* **BIG** *action*

Day Twenty-Seven

Speak Him

> "The soothing tongue is a tree of life,
> but a perverse tongue crushes the spirit."

PROVERBS 15:4

On New Year's Eve, as we entered 2023, I was laying in bed, praying and asking God to speak to me. What I received from Him were the words "Speak Him."

It was so crazy to receive these words because they fully align with what I want to do this year!

You may be thinking that God speaks to me a lot in my bedroom, but that is because I have blessed my room. And it is where I make room for Him to speak to me. You may think I am crazy, but I have prayed over everything in my room because I wanted it to be a place for me to feel closest to God.

The meaning of the words "Speak Him" is so important to me. We speak so many things over ourselves and the people around us that are not of the Lord. It's time to Speak Him! I have had a lot of people Speak Him over me, and I want to start doing that for other people too.

These words are so important to me that I have created a clothing brand around it. I make shirts that say "Speak Him" on them so that we are always reminded that we are made in His image. We are made to Speak Him over our nation and ourselves.

LET'S GET REAL.

Spill the tea:

- *Are you speaking Jesus over yourself?*
- *Are you speaking Him over others?*

BOLD *faith*  **BIG** *action*

Day Twenty-Eight

It Is Time to Multiply

> "To those who use well what they are given, even more will be given, and they will have an abundance. But from those who do nothing, even what little they have will be taken away."
>
> **MATTHEW 25:29**

When I think of multiplying, I think of the Parable of the Three Servants:

"Again, the Kingdom of Heaven can be illustrated by the story of a man going on a long trip. He called together his servants and entrusted his money to them while he was gone. He gave five bags of silver to one, two bags of silver to another, and one bag of silver to the last—dividing it in proportion to their abilities. He then left on his trip.

The servant who received the five bags of silver began to invest the money and earned five more. The servant with two bags of silver also went to work and earned two more. But the servant who received the one bag of silver dug a hole in the ground and hid the master's money." Matthew 25:14–18

When the master returned home, he praised the servants who went to work and made more money, but he punished the servant who had hidden the money in the ground and done nothing.

Those who multiplied were rewarded!

I know people that think that we are supposed to stay where we are, not want more, and just be grateful. But being grateful does not mean settling for less!

The parable continues on to say in Matthew 25:29, "To those who use well what they are given, even more will be given, and they will have an abundance. But from those who do nothing, even what little they have will be taken away."

You were created to have a fulfilling life. God wants to bless you and multiply what you have! He wants you to get everything you could ever think of or imagine. But He can not bless someone that does not want to work for it. Good enough is not what God wants for us.

In the first chapter of Genesis, it says seven times that God said it was good. God saw His creation and said it was good. Not good enough. He said it was good! You do not want just a good enough life.

It's time to do the work, get uncomfortable, and multiply!

LET'S GET REAL.

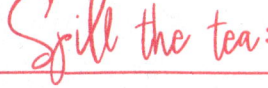

- *Are there areas of your life where you are settling for good enough? What are they?*
- *How can you start multiplying your blessings in your life?*

Day Twenty-Nine

Dripping with the Flavor of God!

> "Finally, be strong in the Lord and in his mighty power. Put on the full armor of God, so that you can take your stand against the devil's schemes."

EPHESIANS 6:10

A couple of weeks ago, I was in chapel class, and the pastor of our school mentioned how we are all dripping with the flavor of God. I immediately thought about how that idea would be the perfect ending chapter of my devotional!

As you have been reading the devotions in this book, I hope you have found yourself dripping with the flavor of God. This could mean many different things.

YES & BLESSED

Maybe you feel God walking with you more. Maybe you are using His word more in your life. Maybe you've put on His armor and feel invincible? Or maybe people even notice that you're changing? Whatever it is, I am so happy for you!

I am so proud of you for finishing this devotional! God will bless you for bettering yourself and being intentional with your time. I want you to know He sees you, and He is so proud of you. You are His child, and He loves you!

Go into your next season saying yes and be ready to be *blessed* ♥.

LET'S GET REAL.

Spill the tea:

- *What will you take away from the 30 days of this devotional?*
- *What will you start doing differently?*

BOLD *faith*  BIG *action*

Day Thirty

Your Final Exercise!

> "I praise you because I am fearfully and wonderfully made; your works are wonderful, I know that full well."
>
> **PSALM 139:14**

For the first thirteen years of my life, I never thought about what made me special. I always thought of myself as different. Instead of that being a positive thing, I thought of it in a negative way. During the last three years of my life, as I have walked through hard times and joyful times, I have found what makes me special.

One of the things that makes me special is that I always try to do the right thing; I never waver from God. Even when I don't know what to do, I choose God over and over again. I also stick to what I feel called to do. In any situation in life, I listen to where I feel called to be.

I also now see that I am special *because* I am different. There will only ever be one of me! I want people to see me as different and know that I am not like everyone else. Over the last three years, I found my voice, and I can stand up for what is right. I bring the light and not the dark. I am the head and not the tail. I am made for a purpose. That's what makes me special!

As the final exercise of this book, I want you to write about what makes you special. What gifts has God given you that the world needs to see? The next time you aren't sure you can make it through, just look at this page and remember God made you, and you are special!

YOUR FINAL EXERCISE!

About the Author

Kihryn Kha is a testament to the boundless potential of youthful spirit, combined with unwavering faith and natural talent. Despite being just sixteen years old and standing at a whopping five feet tall, Kihryn is a powerhouse inspirational figure for her peers and those around her, manifesting her love for Jesus in everything she does!

Kihryn's deep-rooted faith guides her in all aspects of her life. Her devotion is not just expressed in her prayers but also reflected in her actions and commitment to encouraging others on their spiritual journeys.

In a testament to her mature understanding of her faith, she has recently become a published author with *this* devotional, a work that exudes her love for Jesus and offers a spiritual guide to all navigating their way through life's challenges. Kihryn is also a sought-after keynote speaker, delivering a powerful message of faith, boldness, and favor.

On top of these talents, Kihryn is a stellar golfer, an avid music listener, and a loving daughter, sister, and friend. In her free time, she loves to shop, go to youth groups, and paint! One of her life goals is to have three houses: one in Arizona, one at the beach, and one in the Utah mountains.

Get in touch with Kihryn:

Speaking Inquiries
speaking@kihrynkha.com

Follow on Instagram, Facebook, and Tiktok
@KihrynKha

Made in the USA
Columbia, SC
16 August 2023